The Law of God

Second Edition, Revised

Compiled by T. M. Moore

Waxed Tablet Publications
Knoxville, TN

Waxed Tablet Publications
Knoxville, TN
Copyright 2006, 2009 The Fellowship of Ailbe
ISBN: 978-0-578-01685-6

The Law of God

Foreword to the Second Edition

This second edition of *The Law of God* accomplishes three purposes.

First, it corrects simple typographical and editorial errors which were discovered in the first edition. These were not many, but our desire is to have as clean and readable a presentation of God's Law as possible. Consistent with that purpose, we have also made some improvements in the formatting of the material, and we increased the font size for easier reading.

Second, introductory comments to each of the commandments, and each of the sub-sections under the commandments, are intended to help the reader understand the ongoing relevance of the Law of God to contemporary life. The Apostle Paul insisted that, because only Jesus' righteousness suffices to save us, this does not mean that the Law of God has been abolished. Indeed, he declared that the Law has been established as holy and righteous and good for all those who have attained the righteousness of Jesus Christ by grace through faith. We do not keep the Law, in other words, in order to *be* saved, but *for the sake of* salvation, that we may know and enjoy life to the full, as Christ did, and as God intends for us as well (cf. Rom. 3.31; 7.12; 1 Jn. 2.1-6; Lev. 18.1-5).

Third, this edition incorporates references to other passages in the Scriptures where the relevance of a particular law or statute seems to be in view, or where clarification is added in helping to understand the application of the Law for today.

As in the previous edition we have omitted most references to the work of priests – the sacrificial system, protocols for cleansing and healing, and the furnishings of the sanctuary. Jesus Christ, our great and final High Priest, has done away with the work of all previous priests, establishing His own priesthood in the place of that elaborated in the Law, and offering His sacraments in place of the regulations and procedures for approaching God associated with the Old Testament priesthood, the tabernacle, and the temple. In so doing we do not imply that there are no abiding principles to be learned from the ministry of Old Testament priests. Jesus discovered principles for observing the Sabbath in the way David made use of the bread of presence in the tabernacle (Matt. 12.1-8), and Paul discerned a principle for the support of ministers of the Gospel in the way sacrifices were disposed among the priests (1 Cor. 9.12-14). Thus we should not omit reading and meditation in all the Law of God – the first five books of Scripture – for there many excellent insights may be gained for the life of faith and, especially, with respect to the work of our Lord Jesus Christ.

However, in this edition as the first, we have included only the Ten Commandments and the civil laws which pertain to them as of most practical importance for following the path of righteousness that Jesus walked (2 Jn. 2.1-6). A companion volume to this one, *The Ground for Christian Ethics*, takes up in more detail the manner of reading, studying, and using the Law of God in the life of faith today.

The reading and study of God's Law is foundational to understanding all of Scripture. In a very real sense, all the Old Testament beyond the Law of God is an elaboration or explanation of that Law, so much so, in fact, that the New Testament can speak of both the books of the prophets and the sacred writings as the Law of God (cf. 1 Cor. 14.21, Jn. 10.31). And when we consider that Jesus came not to abolish the Law, but to fulfill it, and that those who trust in Him are called to walk as He walked, this makes the reading and study of God's Law important for a right understanding of the New Testament as well (Matt. 5.17-19; 1 Jn. 2.1-6).

Readers of the first edition have found this little compilation to be a useful resource for daily meditation in the Law of God. My personal use of this compilation has been, as part of my morning time of prayer and reading, to meditate on a section or a few verses of a section, reading continually through the Law in an effort better to hide it in my heart (Ps. 1; Ps. 119.9-11). I never cease to be amazed at the way principles and precepts which I contemplate in the Law of God collide with contemporary situations, offering insights into the way the further unfolding of the divine economy may one day redress many of the worlds ills and uncertainties.

The goal of all reading, study, and obedience to the Law of God is love. Indeed, we cannot understand the Law of God apart from a settled conviction to discover within it practical guidance for improving love for God and men (Matt. 22.34-40). Therefore let this be the goal of all reading, meditation, and teaching of the Law of God, for if it is, we may surely expect the blessing of the Lord to attend thereunto (1 Tim. 1.5).

-T. M. Moore
Hamilton, VA

Introduction

The Venerable Bede (c. 673-735), one of the earliest historians of the Celtic Christian revival, relates a wonderful story that demonstrates the important place the Law of God held in the minds of church leaders in that generation.

In an attempt to re-assert Roman authority over the rapidly-growing Celtic Christian movement, Pope Gregory (540-604) dispatched an emissary to England named Augustine (d. 604). Upon arriving, his first duty was to summon the Celtic bishops to meet with him. Those bishops, eager to do the right thing, sought the counsel of one of their esteemed elders concerning what they should do. He told them that, if Augustine was an honorable man, they should submit to him. All well and good, they replied, but how were they to know if he was an honorable man?

The elder counseled them to make sure that Augustine arrived at the meeting first, and was seated when they, the bishops, entered the room. "If he rises to greet you, he is an honorable man, and you can submit to him."

The relevance of this story with respect to the Law of God will shortly be made clear.

Few subjects could be more important for contemporary Christians than the study of the Law of God. Christians have for too long ignored or minimized the Law of God – which, as Paul put it, the Lord has given to guide us in matters "holy and righteous and good" (Rom. 7:12). While almost all Christians agree that the Ten Commandments are important, there is very little agreement, and even less consistent practice, relative to their use in the household of faith. As for the other aspects of the Law, believers today remain largely ignorant of their content and indifferent to their role in the Christian life.

But the Law was given to the people of God by the grace of their Redeemer, so that they might learn to love Him and their neighbors, might enter into the fullness of life and goodness, and might walk in the beauty of holiness, peace, and rest. We ignore the Law of God to our great peril and shame.

The texts of the Law that follow include the two statements of the Ten Commandments (from Exodus and Deuteronomy) together with the various civil codes, arranged topically under the particular commandment to which they seem most to be related. These "case laws", while no longer (in most cases) valid as to their original intent and design, nonetheless contain valuable principles of holiness, righteousness, and goodness which, as we are able to discern them, can guide us in realizing the Lord's plan for a loving community (cf. 1 Cor. 9:8-10). The religious or ceremonial laws of Israel, including the dietary laws and the laws of cleansing, have been omitted from this compilation, as the work of priests related to tabernacle and temple has been superseded and brought to an end by the work of our great High Priest, the Lord Jesus Christ (cf. Heb. 7-10).

This compilation is prepared to give Christians a handy tool for regularly reading through and meditating daily on the Law of God, a practice, David reminds us, which characterizes those who know the Lord and live fruitfully for Him (Ps. 1). Readers may find that a page a day of this compilation provides a manageable diet of God's Law for ongoing personal growth.

The Scriptures liken the Law of God to a mirror, in which we may see a reflection of ourselves, and of the sin that yet remains (Jms. 1:22-25), against the backdrop of God's glory as it radiates out from the Law, focusing us on the face of Jesus, and directing us as to how we may live for God's glory as we are transformed into the very image of Christ by His Spirit (2 Cor. 3:12-18; 4:6). Thus, a threefold format for meditating on the Law is suggested: As you read and meditate on any text, ask yourself, "What do I see of myself, or of people and the world generally?" "How is God's glory reflected?" "How must I live so as to glorify God and reflect Christ in my life?" Reflecting on these questions throughout the day can be an effective way of hiding the Law of God in your heart, so that the sanctifying grace of God can work its transforming power in your soul (Ps. 119:9-11; Jn. 17:17).

As it turned out, Augustine failed to stand when the Celtic bishops entered the room, and merely extended his hand for them to kiss as a sign of submission. By failing to rise he demonstrated, either that he did not *know* the Law of God, which commands deference to elders, demonstrated by rising (Lev. 19:32), or he did not *regard* the Law with the kind of respect that Celtic elders and bishops knew it deserved. By failing to rise in their presence, Augustine postponed for nearly 100 years the entry of the Celtic churches into the Roman Catholic fold.

May the Lord be pleased to use this compilation to help His people learn to love the Law of God and delight in it, meditating on it throughout their days (Ps. 119:97) and finding it to be a lamp unto their feet and a light upon their paths as they grow in love for God and for their neighbors (Ps. 119:105; Mt. 22:34-40).

I would like to thank Misty Keller for her help in compiling these texts and composing the final manuscript, and Reuel Sample, our intrepid web master and director of publications, for preparing it for publication through Waxed Tablet Publications. I also want to thank my wife and editor, Susie, for her careful proofreading and helpful suggestions about the arrangement of the civil laws under their particular commandment.

This compilation is dedicated to the members and friends of The Fellowship of Ailbe, and to all who long to be able to say with full conviction and joy, "O how I love your law!" (Ps. 119.97)

-T. M. Moore
Summer, 2006

1 The First Commandment

No other gods

The Commandment

God, by virtue of His exclusivity and uniqueness, and the grace He has exercised toward those He redeems, demands their exclusive devotion and service.

Exodus 20.2, 3

> "I am the LORD your God, who brought you out of the land of Egypt, out of the house of slavery. You shall have no other gods before me."

Deuteronomy 5.6, 7

> "'I am the LORD your God, who brought you out of the land of Egypt, out of the house of slavery. You shall have no other gods before me.'"

Psalm 73.25

1.1 Be holy to the Lord

The precepts and statutes in this section are designed to teach and reinforce devotion to the Lord. God's people are called to discipline their hearts to love and fear Him, their consciences to prefer and choose Him, and all their practices to serve Him. Thus would they be a people holy to the Lord, separated unto Him for the praise of the glory of His grace.

Deuteronomy 10:12-22

> "And now, Israel, what does the LORD your God require of you, but to fear the LORD your God, to walk in all his ways, to love him, to serve the LORD your God with all your heart and with all your soul, and to keep the commandments and statutes of the LORD, which I am commanding you today for your good? Behold, to the LORD your God belong heaven and the heaven of heavens, the earth with all that is in it. Yet the LORD set his heart in love on your fathers and chose their offspring after them, you above all peoples, as you are this day. Circumcise therefore the foreskin of your heart, and be no longer stubborn. For the LORD your God is God of gods and Lord of lords, the great, the mighty, and the awesome God, who is not partial and takes no bribe. He executes justice for the fatherless and

the widow, and loves the sojourner, giving him food and clothing. Love the sojourner, therefore, for you were sojourners in the land of Egypt. You shall fear the LORD your God. You shall serve him and hold fast to him, and by his name you shall swear. He is your praise. He is your God, who has done for you these great and terrifying things that your eyes have seen. Your fathers went down to Egypt seventy persons, and now the LORD your God has made you as numerous as the stars of heaven."

Matthew 10.28; Luke 1.6; Romans 7.12; 1 John 2.1-6

Deuteronomy 11.1, 2

"You shall therefore love the LORD your God and keep his charge, his statutes, his rules, and his commandments always. And consider today (since I am not speaking to your children who have not known or seen it), consider the discipline of the LORD your God, his greatness, his mighty hand and his outstretched arm…"

John 16.8-11; Hebrews 12.5-11

Deuteronomy 12.32

"Everything that I command you, you shall be careful to do. You shall not add to it or take from it.'"

1 Corinthians 4.6; Revelation 22.18, 19

Deuteronomy 6.1-3

"Now this is the commandment, the statutes and the rules that the LORD your God commanded me to teach you, that you may do them in the land to which you are going over, to possess it, that you may fear the LORD your God, you and your son and your son's son, by keeping all his statutes and his commandments, which I command you, all the days of your life, and that your days may be long. Hear therefore, O Israel, and be careful to do them, that it may go well with you, and that you may multiply greatly, as the LORD, the God of your fathers, has promised you, in a land flowing with milk and honey."

Luke 1.6; Ephesians 6.1-3; James 1.22-25

Deuteronomy 6.4-9

"Hear, O Israel: The LORD our God, the LORD is one. You shall love the LORD your God with all your heart and with all your soul and with all your might. And these words that I command you today shall be on your heart. You shall teach them diligently to your children, and shall talk of them when you sit in your house, and when you walk by the way, and when you lie down, and when you rise. You shall bind them as a sign on your hand, and they shall be as frontlets between your eyes. You shall write them on the doorposts of your house and on your gates."

Ephesians 5.15-17; Colossians 4.6

Deuteronomy 6.20-25

"When your son asks you in time to come, 'What is the meaning of the testimonies and the statutes and the rules that the LORD our God has commanded you?' then you shall say to your son, 'We were Pharaoh's slaves in Egypt. And the LORD brought us out of Egypt with a mighty hand. And the LORD showed signs and wonders, great and grievous, against Egypt and against Pharaoh and all his household, before our eyes. And he brought us out from there, that he might bring us in and give us the land that he swore to give to our fathers. And the LORD commanded us to do all these statutes, to fear the LORD our God, for our good always, that he might preserve us alive, as we are this day. And it will be righteousness for us, if we are careful to do all this commandment before the LORD our God, as he has commanded us.'"

Ephesians 2.1-10; Philippians 1.9-11

Deuteronomy 31.9-13

Then Moses wrote this law and gave it to the priests, the sons of Levi, who carried the ark of the covenant of the LORD, and to all the elders of Israel. And Moses commanded them, "At the end of every seven years, at the set time in the year of release, at the Feast of Booths, when all Israel comes to appear before the LORD your God at the place that he will choose, you shall read this law before all Israel in their hearing. Assemble the people, men, women, and little ones, and the sojourner within your towns, that they may hear and learn to fear the LORD your God, and be careful to do all the words of this law, and that their children, who have not known it, may hear and learn to fear the LORD your God, as long as you live in the land that you are going over the Jordan to possess."

Acts 20.26; 2 Timothy 3.15-17

Leviticus 19.2

"Speak to all the congregation of the people of Israel and say to them, You shall be holy, for I the LORD your God am holy."

Matthew 5.44, 45

Leviticus 18.1-5

And the LORD spoke to Moses, saying, "Speak to the people of Israel and say to them, I am the LORD your God. You shall not do as they do in the land of Egypt, where you lived, and you shall not do as they do in the land of Canaan, to which I am bringing you. You shall not walk in their statutes. You shall follow my rules and keep my statutes and walk in them. I am the LORD your God. You shall therefore keep my statutes and my rules; if a person does them, he shall live by them: I am the LORD."

Deuteronomy 32.45-47

And when Moses had finished speaking all these words to Israel, he said to them, "Take to heart all the words by which I am warning you today, that you may command them to your children, that they may be careful to do all the words of this law. For it is no empty word for you, but your very life, and by this word you shall live long in the land that you are going over the Jordan to possess."

Leviticus 20.22-26

"You shall therefore keep all my statutes and all my rules and do them, that the land where I am bringing you to live may not vomit you out. And you shall not walk in the customs of the nation that I am driving out before you, for they did all these things, and therefore I detested them. But I have said to you, 'You shall inherit their land, and I will give it to you to possess, a land flowing with milk and honey.' I am the LORD your God, who have separated you from the peoples. You shall therefore separate the clean beast from the unclean, and the unclean bird from the clean. You shall not make yourselves detestable by beast or by bird or by anything with which the ground crawls, which I have set apart for you to hold unclean. You shall be holy to me, for I the LORD am holy and have separated you from the peoples, that you should be mine."

Leviticus 19.19

"You shall keep my statutes. You shall not let your cattle breed with a different kind. You shall not sow your field with two kinds of seed, nor shall you wear a garment of cloth made of two kinds of material."

Deuteronomy 22.9-11

"You shall not sow your vineyard with two kinds of seed, lest the whole yield be forfeited, the crop that you have sown and the yield of the vineyard. You shall not plow with an ox and a donkey together. You shall not wear cloth of wool and linen mixed together."

Leviticus 19.23-25

"When you come into the land and plant any kind of tree for food, then you shall regard its fruit as forbidden. Three years it shall be forbidden to you; it must not be eaten. And in the fourth year all its fruit shall be holy, an offering of praise to the LORD. But in the fifth year you may eat of its fruit, to increase its yield for you: I am the LORD your God."

Deuteronomy 23.12-14

"You shall have a place outside the camp, and you shall go out to it. And you shall have a trowel with your tools, and when you sit down outside, you shall dig a hole with it and turn back and cover up your excrement. Because the LORD your God walks in the midst of your camp, to deliver you and to give up your enemies before you, therefore your camp must be holy, so that he may not see anything indecent among you and turn away from you."

Exodus 22.31

"You shall be consecrated to me. Therefore you shall not eat any flesh that is torn by beasts in the field; you shall throw it to the dogs."

1.2 Honor no other gods

God's people are to honor no other gods – no other ultimate sources of counsel or truth, and no other objects of veneration or devotion. They must guard against any inclination to turn to other gods or other counselors; He alone must be their God.

Deuteronomy 6.13-15

> "It is the LORD your God you shall fear. Him you shall serve and by his name you shall swear. You shall not go after other gods, the gods of the peoples who are around you, for the LORD your God in your midst is a jealous God, lest the anger of the LORD your God be kindled against you, and he destroy you from off the face of the earth."

Exodus 23.13

> "Pay attention to all that I have said to you, and make no mention of the names of other gods, nor let it be heard on your lips."

Exodus 22.20

> "Whoever sacrifices to any god, other than the LORD alone, shall be devoted to destruction."

Deuteronomy 17.2-7

> "If there is found among you, within any of your towns that the LORD your God is giving you, a man or woman who does what is evil in the sight of the LORD your God, in transgressing his covenant, and has gone and served other gods and worshiped them, or the sun or the moon or any of the host of heaven, which I have forbidden, and it is told you and you hear of it, then you shall inquire diligently, and if it is true and certain that such an abomination has been done in Israel, then you shall bring out to your gates that man or woman who has done this evil thing, and you shall stone that man or woman to death with stones. On the evidence of two witnesses or of three witnesses the one who is to die shall be put to death; a person shall not be put to death on the evidence of one witness. The hand of the witnesses shall be first against him to put him to death, and afterward the hand of all the people. So you shall purge the evil from your midst."

Deuteronomy 23.17-18

> "None of the daughters of Israel shall be a cult prostitute, and none of the sons of Israel shall be a cult prostitute. You shall not bring the fee of a prostitute or the wages of a dog into the house of the LORD your God in payment for any vow, for both of these are an abomination to the LORD your God."

Leviticus 19.31

> "Do not turn to mediums or wizards; do not seek them out, and so make yourselves unclean by them: I am the LORD your God."

Isaiah 8.19, 20; Acts 16.16-18

Leviticus 20.6

> "If a person turns to mediums and wizards, whoring after them, I will set my face against that person and will cut him off from among his people."

Exodus 22.18

> "You shall not permit a sorceress to live."

Leviticus 20.27

> "A man or a woman who is a medium or a wizard shall surely be put to death. They shall be stoned with stones; their blood shall be upon them."

1.3 Exercise stewardship unto the Lord

Believers are called to be good stewards unto the Lord, to use their personal property as a way of demonstrating and reinforcing their separateness unto the Lord. The tithe, the selling and redeeming of the land,, and the practice of devoting things to the Lord all provided ways for the Lord to remind His people that the earth and everything in it are His, and that they must express in tangible ways that they are a people holy to the Lord.

Leviticus 25.23, 24

> "The land shall not be sold in perpetuity, for the land is mine. For you are strangers and sojourners with me. And in all the country you possess, you shall allow a redemption of the land."

Leviticus 25.25-28

"If your brother becomes poor and sells part of his property, then his nearest redeemer shall come and redeem what his brother has sold. If a man has no one to redeem it and then himself becomes prosperous and finds sufficient means to redeem it, let him calculate the years since he sold it and pay back the balance to the man to whom he sold it, and then return to his property. But if he has not sufficient means to recover it, then what he sold shall remain in the hand of the buyer until the year of jubilee. In the jubilee it shall be released, and he shall return to his property."

Leviticus 25.29-34

"If a man sells a dwelling house in a walled city, he may redeem it within a year of its sale. For a full year he shall have the right of redemption. If it is not redeemed within a full year, then the house in the walled city shall belong in perpetuity to the buyer, throughout his generations; it shall not be released in the jubilee. But the houses of the villages that have no wall around them shall be classified with the fields of the land. They may be redeemed, and they shall be released in the jubilee. As for the cities of the Levites, the Levites may redeem at any time the houses in the cities they possess. And if one of the Levites exercises his right of redemption, then the house that was sold in a city they possess shall be released in the jubilee. For the houses in the cities of the Levites are their possession among the people of Israel. But the fields of pastureland belonging to their cities may not be sold, for that is their possession forever."

Leviticus 27.30-33

"Every tithe of the land, whether of the seed of the land or of the fruit of the trees, is the LORD's; it is holy to the LORD. If a man wishes to redeem some of his tithe, he shall add a fifth to it. [32]And every tithe of herds and flocks, every tenth animal of all that pass under the herdsman's staff, shall be holy to the LORD. One shall not differentiate between good or bad, neither shall he make a substitute for it; and if he does substitute for it, then both it and the substitute shall be holy; it shall not be redeemed."

Leviticus 22.1-3; 1 Corinthians 9.16-21

Exodus 22.29

"You shall not delay to offer from the fullness of your harvest and from the outflow of your presses. The firstborn of your sons you shall give to me."

Numbers 3.11-13

Exodus 23.19

> "The best of the firstfruits of your ground you shall bring into the house
> of the LORD your God."

Proverbs 3.9, 10

Deuteronomy 14.22, 23

> "You shall tithe all the yield of your seed that comes from the field year by
> year. And before the LORD your God, in the place that he will choose, to
> make his name dwell there, you shall eat the tithe of your grain, of your
> wine, and of your oil, and the firstborn of your herd and flock, that you
> may learn to fear the LORD your God always."

Deuteronomy 26.12-15

> "When you have finished paying all the tithe of your produce in the third
> year, which is the year of tithing, giving it to the Levite, the sojourner, the
> fatherless, and the widow, so that they may eat within your towns and be
> filled, then you shall say before the LORD your God, 'I have removed the
> sacred portion out of my house, and moreover, I have given it to the
> Levite, the sojourner, the fatherless, and the widow, according to all your
> commandment that you have commanded me. I have not transgressed any
> of your commandments, nor have I forgotten them. I have not eaten of
> the tithe while I was mourning, or removed any of it while I was unclean,
> or offered any of it to the dead. I have obeyed the voice of the LORD my
> God. I have done according to all that you have commanded me. Look
> down from your holy habitation, from heaven, and bless your people Israel
> and the ground that you have given us, as you swore to our fathers, a land
> flowing with milk and honey.'"

Leviticus 27.28, 29

> "But no devoted thing that a man devotes to the LORD, of anything that
> he has, whether man or beast, or of his inherited field, shall be sold or
> redeemed; every devoted thing is most holy to the LORD. No one
> devoted, who is to be devoted for destruction from mankind, shall be
> ransomed; he shall surely be put to death."

First Commandment

Matthew 26.6-13

Leviticus 27.1-8

> The LORD spoke to Moses, saying, "Speak to the people of Israel and say
> to them, If anyone makes a special vow to the LORD involving the
> valuation of persons, then the valuation of a male from twenty years old up
> to sixty years old shall be fifty shekels of silver, according to the shekel of
> the sanctuary. If the person is a female, the valuation shall be thirty
> shekels. If the person is from five years old up to twenty years old, the
> valuation shall be for a male twenty shekels, and for a female ten shekels. If
> the person is from a month old up to five years old, the valuation shall be
> for a male five shekels of silver, and for a female the valuation shall be
> three shekels of silver. And if the person is sixty years old or over, then the
> valuation for a male shall be fifteen shekels, and for a female ten shekels.
> And if someone is too poor to pay the valuation, then he shall be made to
> stand before the priest, and the priest shall value him; the priest shall value
> him according to what the vower can afford."

2 Kings 12.4-8

Leviticus 27.9-13

> "If the vow is an animal that may be offered as an offering to the LORD,
> all of it that he gives to the LORD is holy. He shall not exchange it or make
> a substitute for it, good for bad, or bad for good; and if he does in fact
> substitute one animal for another, then both it and the substitute shall be
> holy. And if it is any unclean animal that may not be offered as an offering
> to the LORD, then he shall stand the animal before the priest, and the
> priest shall value it as either good or bad; as the priest values it, so it shall
> be. But if he wishes to redeem it, he shall add a fifth to the valuation."

Leviticus 27.14, 15

> "When a man dedicates his house as a holy gift to the LORD, the priest
> shall value it as either good or bad; as the priest values it, so it shall stand.
> [1]And if the donor wishes to redeem his house, he shall add a fifth to the
> valuation price, and it shall be his."

Leviticus 27.16-25

"If a man dedicates to the LORD part of the land that is his possession, then the valuation shall be in proportion to its seed. A homer of barley seed shall be valued at fifty shekels of silver. If he dedicates his field from the year of jubilee, the valuation shall stand, but if he dedicates his field after the jubilee, then the priest shall calculate the price according to the years that remain until the year of jubilee, and a deduction shall be made from the valuation. And if he who dedicates the field wishes to redeem it, then he shall add a fifth to its valuation price, and it shall remain his. But if he does not wish to redeem the field, or if he has sold the field to another man, it shall not be redeemed anymore. But the field, when it is released in the jubilee, shall be a holy gift to the LORD, like a field that has been devoted. The priest shall be in possession of it. If he dedicates to the LORD a field that he has bought, which is not a part of his possession, then the priest shall calculate the amount of the valuation for it up to the year of jubilee, and the man shall give the valuation on that day as a holy gift to the LORD. In the year of jubilee the field shall return to him from whom it was bought, to whom the land belongs as a possession. Every valuation shall be according to the shekel of the sanctuary: twenty gerahs shall make a shekel."

2 Samuel 24.18-24

Leviticus 27.26, 27

"But a firstborn of animals, which as a firstborn belongs to the LORD, no man may dedicate; whether ox or sheep, it is the LORD's. And if it is an unclean animal, then he shall buy it back at the valuation, and add a fifth to it; or, if it is not redeemed, it shall be sold at the valuation."

2   The Second Commandment

No images

The Commandment

God is holy, and He calls His people to be holy by worshiping and serving Him only. He will allow no admixture of pagan practices in the worship and service of His Name, nothing that reduces His immensity, restricts His sovereignty, compromises His holiness, obscures His uniqueness, or otherwise profanes His Name.

Exodus 20.4-6

> "You shall not make for yourself a carved image, or any likeness of anything that is in heaven above, or that is in the earth beneath, or that is in the water under the earth. You shall not bow down to them or serve them, for I the LORD your God am a jealous God, visiting the iniquity of the fathers on the children to the third and the fourth generation of those who hate me, but showing steadfast love to thousands of those who love me and keep my commandments."

Deuteronomy 5.8-10

> "'You shall not make for yourself a carved image, or any likeness of anything that is in heaven above, or that is on the earth beneath, or that is in the water under the earth. You shall not bow down to them or serve them; for I the LORD your God am a jealous God, visiting the iniquity of the fathers on the children to the third and fourth generation of those who hate me, but showing steadfast love to thousands of those who love me and keep my commandments.'"

1 Corinthians 10.14; 1 John 5.21

2.1 Worship God's way

The worship of God is not to be conducted with pagan ways or practices. All elements of pagan worship are to be excluded from the worship of God, Who is holy and pure, and Who shows us how to worship Him as we ought.

Exodus 23.23-25, 32, 33

> "When my angel goes before you and brings you to the Amorites and the Hittites and the Perizzites and the Canaanites, the Hivites and the Jebusites, and I blot them out, you shall not bow down to their gods nor serve them, nor do as they do, but you shall utterly overthrow them and break their pillars in pieces. You shall serve the LORD your God, and he will bless your bread and your water, and I will take sickness away from among you... You shall make no covenant with them and their gods... They shall not dwell in your land, lest they make you sin against me; for if you serve their gods, it will surely be a snare to you."

2 Corinthians 10.3-5; Numbers 33.50-52

Deuteronomy 12.2-4

> "You shall surely destroy all the places where the nations whom you shall dispossess served their gods, on the high mountains and on the hills and under every green tree. You shall tear down their altars and dash in pieces their pillars and burn their Asherim with fire. You shall chop down the carved images of their gods and destroy their name out of that place. You shall not worship the LORD your God in that way."

Acts 19.18, 19

Deuteronomy 12.29-31

> "When the LORD your God cuts off before you the nations whom you go in to dispossess, and you dispossess them and dwell in their land, take care that you be not ensnared to follow them, after they have been destroyed before you, and that you do not inquire about their gods, saying, 'How did these nations serve their gods? – that I also may do the same.' You shall not worship the LORD your God in that way, for every abominable thing that the LORD hates they have done for their gods, for they even burn their sons and their daughters in the fire to their gods."

2.2 Guard against being drawn away

We must beware of those who would lead us away from the Lord, and we must prove our love for Him by resisting their allurements and clinging in love and fear to the Lord alone.

Deuteronomy 13.1-5

"If a prophet or a dreamer of dreams arises among you and gives you a sign or a wonder, and the sign or wonder that he tells you comes to pass, and if he says, 'Let us go after other gods,' which you have not known, 'and let us serve them,' you shall not listen to the words of that prophet or that dreamer of dreams. For the LORD your God is testing you, to know whether you love the LORD your God with all your heart and with all your soul. You shall walk after the LORD your God and fear him and keep his commandments and obey his voice, and you shall serve him and hold fast to him. But that prophet or that dreamer of dreams shall be put to death, because he has taught rebellion against the LORD your God, who brought you out of the land of Egypt and redeemed you out of the house of slavery, to make you leave the way in which the LORD your God commanded you to walk. So you shall purge the evil from your midst."

Galatians 1.8, 9

Deuteronomy 13.6-11

"If your brother, the son of your mother, or your son or your daughter or the wife you embrace or your friend who is as your own soul entices you secretly, saying, 'Let us go and serve other gods,' which neither you nor your fathers have known, some of the gods of the peoples who are around you, whether near you or far off from you, from the one end of the earth to the other, you shall not yield to him or listen to him, nor shall your eye pity him, nor shall you spare him, nor shall you conceal him. But you shall kill him. Your hand shall be first against him to put him to death, and afterward the hand of all the people. You shall stone him to death with stones, because he sought to draw you away from the LORD your God, who brought you out of the land of Egypt, out of the house of slavery. And all Israel shall hear and fear and never again do any such wickedness as this among you."

Deuteronomy 13.12-18

> "If you hear in one of your cities, which the LORD your God is giving you to dwell there, that certain worthless fellows have gone out among you and have drawn away the inhabitants of their city, saying, 'Let us go and serve other gods,' which you have not known, then you shall inquire and make search and ask diligently. And behold, if it be true and certain that such an abomination has been done among you, you shall surely put the inhabitants of that city to the sword, devoting it to destruction, all who are in it and its cattle, with the edge of the sword. You shall gather all its spoil into the midst of its open square and burn the city and all its spoil with fire, as a whole burnt offering to the LORD your God. It shall be a heap forever. It shall not be built again. None of the devoted things shall stick to your hand, that the LORD may turn from the fierceness of his anger and show you mercy and have compassion on you and multiply you, as he swore to your fathers, if you obey the voice of the LORD your God, keeping all his commandments that I am commanding you today, and doing what is right in the sight of the LORD your God."

2.3 Make no idols

God commands us to find Him and Him alone all-sufficient for our needs, and thus to focus all our worship and devotion on Him, and to give none to idols.

Exodus 20.23

> "You shall not make gods of silver to be with me, nor shall you make for yourselves gods of gold."

Exodus 34.17

> "You shall not make for yourself any gods of cast metal."

Leviticus 19.4

> "Do not turn to idols or make for yourselves any gods of cast metal: I am the LORD your God."

Leviticus 26.1

> "You shall not make idols for yourselves or erect an image or pillar, and you shall not set up a figured stone in your land to bow down to it, for I am the LORD your God."

2.4 Reject pagan practices

God's people must not adopt, for any reason, the harmful, disgusting practices of the pagan peoples they are called to displace.

Leviticus 18.21

> "You shall not give any of your children to offer them to Molech, and so profane the name of your God: I am the LORD."

Leviticus 20.1-5

> The LORD spoke to Moses, saying, "Say to the people of Israel, Any one of the people of Israel or of the strangers who sojourn in Israel who gives any of his children to Molech shall surely be put to death. The people of the land shall stone him with stones. I myself will set my face against that man and will cut him off from among his people, because he has given one of his children to Molech, to make my sanctuary unclean and to profane my holy name. And if the people of the land do at all close their eyes to that man when he gives one of his children to Molech, and do not put him to death, then I will set my face against that man and against his clan and will cut them off from among their people, him and all who follow him in whoring after Molech."

Deuteronomy 18.9-13

> "When you come into the land that the LORD your God is giving you, you shall not learn to follow the abominable practices of those nations. There shall not be found among you anyone who burns his son or his daughter as an offering, anyone who practices divination or tells fortunes or interprets omens, or a sorcerer or a charmer or a medium or a wizard or a necromancer, for whoever does these things is an abomination to the LORD. And because of these abominations the LORD your God is driving them out before you. You shall be blameless before the LORD your God…"

Leviticus 19.26-28

> "You shall not eat any flesh with the blood in it. You shall not interpret omens or tell fortunes. You shall not round off the hair on your temples or mar the edges of your beard. You shall not make any cuts on your body for the dead or tattoo yourselves: I am the LORD."

3   The Third Commandment

Do not take the LORD's name in vain

The Commandment

God invites us to take His Name upon us, to be reconciled to Him and united with Him for the purpose of His glory and their blessedness. We must not take His Name in any way other than what will fulfill these purposes, and we must not vow empty or unwise vows in His Name.

Exodus 20.7

> "You shall not take the name of the LORD your God in vain, for the LORD will not hold him guiltless who takes his name in vain."

Deuteronomy 5.11

> "'You shall not take the name of the LORD your God in vain, for the LORD will not hold him guiltless who takes his name in vain.'"

1 Corinthians 15.1, 2; 1 Corinthians 15.58; 2 Corinthians 6.1; Galatians 4.8-11; James 1.26

3.1 Do not sin against God's Name

Preserve the holiness of God's Name by not bringing it down through falsehood, cursing, or blasphemy.

Leviticus 19.12

> "You shall not swear by my name falsely, and so profane the name of your God: I am the LORD."

Leviticus 24.15, 16

> "And speak to the people of Israel, saying, Whoever curses his God shall bear his sin. Whoever blasphemes the name of the LORD shall surely be put to death. All the congregation shall stone him. The sojourner as well as the native, when he blasphemes the Name, shall be put to death."

3.2 Fulfill your vows

Since the vows we take in some ways mirror the covenant oath of the Lord, we must be careful to fulfill all our vows; we may only be released from vows by proper authorities.

Numbers 30.1, 2

> Moses spoke to the heads of the tribes of the people of Israel, saying, "This is what the LORD has commanded. If a man vows a vow to the LORD, or swears an oath to bind himself by a pledge, he shall not break his word. He shall do according to all that proceeds out of his mouth."

Deuteronomy 23.21-23; Ecclesiastes 5.4-6

Numbers 30.3-5

> "If a woman vows a vow to the LORD and binds herself by a pledge, while within her father's house in her youth, and her father hears of her vow and of her pledge by which she has bound herself and says nothing to her, then all her vows shall stand, and every pledge by which she has bound herself shall stand. But if her father opposes her on the day that he hears of it, no vow of hers, no pledge by which she has bound herself shall stand. And the LORD will forgive her, because her father opposed her."

Numbers 30.6-15

> "If she marries a husband, while under her vows or any thoughtless utterance of her lips by which she has bound herself, and her husband hears of it and says nothing to her on the day that he hears, then her vows shall stand, and her pledges by which she has bound herself shall stand. But if, on the day that her husband comes to hear of it, he opposes her, then he makes void her vow that was on her, and the thoughtless utterance of her lips by which she bound herself. And the LORD will forgive her. (But any vow of a widow or of a divorced woman, anything by which she has bound herself, shall stand against her.) And if she vowed in her husband's house or bound herself by a pledge with an oath, and her husband heard of it and said nothing to her and did not oppose her, then all her vows shall stand, and every pledge by which she bound herself shall stand. But if her husband makes them null and void on the day that he hears them, then whatever proceeds out of her lips concerning her vows or concerning her pledge of herself shall not stand. Her husband has made them void, and the LORD will forgive her. Any vow and any binding oath

to afflict herself, her husband may establish, or her husband may make void. But if her husband says nothing to her from day to day, then he establishes all her vows or all her pledges that are upon her. He has established them, because he said nothing to her on the day that he heard of them. But if he makes them null and void after he has heard of them, then he shall bear her iniquity."

4   The Fourth Commandment

Remember the Sabbath to keep it holy

The Commandment

God commands solemn rest for His people, times when they are to withdraw from their normal practices of work to be with Him in worship, meditation, giving, and remembering. We are carefully to guard and observe these times of rest, so that we may remember the sovereign power and redeeming grace of our God, and give Him the worship and obedience which are His due.

Exodus 20.8-11

> "Remember the Sabbath day, to keep it holy. Six days you shall labor, and do all your work, but the seventh day is a Sabbath to the LORD your God. On it you shall not do any work, you, or your son, or your daughter, your male servant, or your female servant, or your livestock, or the sojourner who is within your gates. For in six days the LORD made heaven and earth, the sea, and all that is in them, and rested the seventh day. Therefore the LORD blessed the Sabbath day and made it holy."

Deuteronomy 5.12-15

> "'Observe the Sabbath day, to keep it holy, as the LORD your God commanded you. Six days you shall labor and do all your work, but the seventh day is a Sabbath to the LORD your God. On it you shall not do any work, you or your son or your daughter or your male servant or your female servant, or your ox or your donkey or any of your livestock, or the sojourner who is within your gates, that your male servant and your female servant may rest as well as you. You shall remember that you were a slave in the land of Egypt, and the LORD your God brought you out from there with a mighty hand and an outstretched arm. Therefore the LORD your God commanded you to keep the Sabbath day.'"

Isaiah 56.1-8; Isaiah 58.13, 14

4.1 Observe the Sabbath perpetually

The Sabbath is a sign of our being made holy to the Lord. Keeping it is of the highest priority for all the generations of God's people.

Exodus 31.12-17

> And the LORD said to Moses, "You are to speak to the people of Israel and say, 'Above all you shall keep my Sabbaths, for this is a sign between me and you throughout your generations, that you may know that I, the LORD, sanctify you. You shall keep the Sabbath, because it is holy for you. Everyone who profanes it shall be put to death. Whoever does any work on it, that soul shall be cut off from among his people. Six days shall work be done, but the seventh day is a Sabbath of solemn rest, holy to the LORD. Whoever does any work on the Sabbath day shall be put to death. Therefore the people of Israel shall keep the Sabbath, observing the Sabbath throughout their generations, as a covenant forever. It is a sign forever between me and the people of Israel that in six days the LORD made heaven and earth, and on the seventh day he rested and was refreshed.'"

4.2 Observe sacred rest

We are to observe holy, special rest on the Sabbath, and to encourage all others to do so as well.

Leviticus 23.3

> "Six days shall work be done, but on the seventh day is a Sabbath of solemn rest, a holy convocation. You shall do no work. It is a Sabbath to the LORD in all your dwelling places."

Matthew 12.1-8; Luke 14.1-6

Exodus 34.21

> "Six days you shall work, but on the seventh day you shall rest. In plowing time and in harvest you shall rest."

Exodus 23.12

> "Six days you shall do your work, but on the seventh day you shall rest; that your ox and your donkey may have rest, and the son of your servant woman, and the alien, may be refreshed."

Exodus 35.2, 3

> "Six days work shall be done, but on the seventh day you shall have a Sabbath of solemn rest, holy to the LORD. Whoever does any work on it shall be put to death. You shall kindle no fire in all your dwelling places on the Sabbath day."

4.3 Observe holy convocations

God's people must take care to assemble regularly to worship Him both on His appointed Sabbaths and at the annual feasts, where they celebrate His sovereign and saving grace and daily provision of their needs.

Leviticus 19.3

> "…and you shall keep my Sabbaths: I am the LORD your God. "

Leviticus 19.30

> "You shall keep my Sabbaths and reverence my sanctuary: I am the LORD."

Leviticus 26.2

> "You shall keep my Sabbaths and reverence my sanctuary: I am the LORD."

Leviticus 23:4-6

> "These are the appointed feasts of the LORD, the holy convocations, which you shall proclaim at the time appointed for them. In the first month, on the fourteenth day of the month at twilight, is the LORD's Passover. And on the fifteenth day of the same month is the Feast of Unleavened bread to the LORD; for seven days you shall eat unleavened bread."

Exodus 23.14-17

"Three times in the year you shall keep a feast to me. You shall keep the Feast of Unleavened Bread. As I commanded you, you shall eat unleavened bread for seven days at the appointed time in the month of Abib, for in it you came out of Egypt. None shall appear before me empty-handed. You shall keep the Feast of Harvest, of the firstfruits of your labor, of what you sow in the field. You shall keep the Feast of Ingathering at the end of the year, when you gather in from the field the fruit of your labor. Three times in the year shall all your males appear before the Lord GOD."

Exodus 34.22-24

"You shall observe the Feast of Weeks, the firstfruits of wheat harvest, and the Feast of Ingathering at the year's end. Three times in the year shall all your males appear before the LORD God, the God of Israel. For I will cast out nations before you and enlarge your borders; no one shall covet your land, when you go up to appear before the LORD your God three times in the year."

Leviticus 23.9-11

And the LORD spoke to Moses, saying, "Speak to the people of Israel and say to them, When you come into the land that I give you and reap its harvest, you shall bring the sheaf of the firstfruits of your harvest to the priest, and he shall wave the sheaf before the LORD, so that you may be accepted. On the day after the Sabbath the priest shall wave it."

Leviticus 23.15, 16

"You shall count seven full weeks from the day after the Sabbath, from the day that you brought the sheaf of the wave offering. You shall count fifty days to the day after the seventh Sabbath. Then you shall present a grain offering of new grain to the LORD."

4.4 Observe Sabbath years

By Sabbath and Jubilee years, God reminded the people of His sovereign ownership and provision, of their need to trust in him, and of their duty to the creation and one another.

Leviticus 25.1-7

> The LORD spoke to Moses on Mount Sinai, saying, "Speak to the people of Israel and say to them, When you come into the land that I give you, the land shall keep a Sabbath to the LORD. For six years you shall sow your field, and for six years you shall prune your vineyard and gather in its fruits, but in the seventh year there shall be a Sabbath of solemn rest for the land, a Sabbath to the LORD. You shall not sow your field or prune your vineyard. You shall not reap what grows of itself in your harvest, or gather the grapes of your undressed vine. It shall be a year of solemn rest for the land. The Sabbath of the land shall provide food for you, for yourself and for your male and female slaves and for your hired servant and the sojourner who lives with you, and for your cattle and for the wild animals that are in your land: all its yield shall be for food."

Deuteronomy 15.1-6

> "At the end of every seven years you shall grant a release. And this is the manner of the release: every creditor shall release what he has lent to his neighbor. He shall not exact it of his neighbor, his brother, because the LORD's release has been proclaimed. Of a foreigner you may exact it, but whatever of yours is with your brother your hand shall release. But there will be no poor among you; for the LORD will bless you in the land that the LORD your God is giving you for an inheritance to possess – if only you will strictly obey the voice of the LORD your God, being careful to do all this commandment that I command you today. For the LORD your God will bless you, as he promised you, and you shall lend to many nations, but you shall not borrow, and you shall rule over many nations, but they shall not rule over you."

Acts 4.34, 35

Leviticus 25.8-22

> "You shall count seven weeks of years, seven times seven years, so that the time of the seven weeks of years shall give you forty-nine years. Then you shall sound the loud trumpet on the tenth day of the seventh month. On

the Day of Atonement you shall sound the trumpet throughout all your land. And you shall consecrate the fiftieth year, and proclaim liberty throughout the land to all its inhabitants. It shall be a jubilee for you, when each of you shall return to his property and each of you shall return to his clan. That fiftieth year shall be a jubilee for you; in it you shall neither sow nor reap what grows of itself nor gather the grapes from the undressed vines. For it is a jubilee. It shall be holy to you. You may eat the produce of the field.

"In this year of jubilee each of you shall return to his property. And if you make a sale to your neighbor or buy from your neighbor, you shall not wrong one another. You shall pay your neighbor according to the number of years after the jubilee, and he shall sell to you according to the number of years for crops. If the years are many, you shall increase the price, and if the years are few, you shall reduce the price, for it is the number of the crops that he is selling to you. You shall not wrong one another, but you shall fear your God, for I am the LORD your God.

"Therefore you shall do my statutes and keep my rules and perform them, and then you will dwell in the land securely. The land will yield its fruit, and you will eat your fill and dwell in it securely. And if you say, 'What shall we eat in the seventh year, if we may not sow or gather in our crop?' I will command my blessing on you in the sixth year, so that it will produce a crop sufficient for three years. When you sow in the eighth year, you will be eating some of the old crop; you shall eat the old until the ninth year, when its crop arrives."

5   The Fifth Commandment

Honor your father and your mother

The Commandment

We are called to observe, respect, and honor the God-ordained order of the cosmos, beginning with honoring our parents, and extending to all properly-constituted authorities and powers, others, and the creation itself.

Exodus 20.12

> "Honor your father and your mother, that your days may be long in the land that the LORD your God is giving you."

Deuteronomy 5.16

> "'Honor your father and your mother, as the LORD your God commanded you, that your days may be long, and that it may go well with you in the land that the LORD your God is giving you.'"

5.1 Honor your parents

God's people must hold their parents in high regard and not allow any evil thought or practice to affect this most basic social relationship.

Leviticus 19.3

> "Every one of you shall revere his mother and his father…"

Exodus 21.17

> "Whoever curses his father or his mother shall be put to death."

Mark 7.9-13

Leviticus 20.9

> "For anyone who curses his father or his mother shall surely be put to death; he has cursed his father or his mother; his blood is upon him."

Deuteronomy 21.18-21

"If a man has a stubborn and rebellious son who will not obey the voice of
his father or the voice of his mother, and, though they discipline him, will
not listen to them, then his father and his mother shall take hold of him
and bring him out to the elders of his city at the gate of the place where he
lives, and they shall say to the elders of his city, 'This our son is stubborn
and rebellious; he will not obey our voice; he is a glutton and a drunkard.'
Then all the men of the city shall stone him to death with stones. So you
shall purge the evil from your midst, and all Israel shall hear, and fear."

Exodus 21.15

"Whoever strikes his father or his mother shall be put to death."

5.2 Honor God's Prophet and His prophets

*Hear and obey those who speak God's Word in the tradition of Moses, the prophets, the
Lord Jesus Christ, and the apostles.*

Deuteronomy 18.15-20

"The LORD your God will raise up for you a prophet like me from among
you, from your brothers – it is to him you shall listen – just as you desired
of the LORD your God at Horeb on the day of the assembly, when you
said, 'Let me not hear again the voice of the LORD my God or see this
great fire any more, lest I die.' And the LORD said to me, 'They are right in
what they have spoken. I will raise up for them a prophet like you from
among their brothers. And I will put my words in his mouth, and he shall
speak to them all that I command him. And whoever will not listen to my
words that he shall speak in my name, I myself will require it of him. But
the prophet who presumes to speak a word in my name that I have not
commanded him to speak, or who speaks in the name of other gods, that
same prophet shall die.'"

Romans 15.4; 1 Corinthians 4.6; 2 Corinthians 3.12-18; 1 John 2.1-6

5.3 Honor authorities

The rulers of God's people are called to exercise just judgment, and they are to be honored and obeyed.

Exodus 22.28

"You shall not revile God, nor curse a ruler of your people."

Acts 23.1-5; Romans 13.5; Titus 3.1

Deuteronomy 16.18-20

"You shall appoint judges and officers in all your towns that the LORD your God is giving you, according to your tribes, and they shall judge the people with righteous judgment. You shall not pervert justice. You shall not show partiality, and you shall not accept a bribe, for a bribe blinds the eyes of the wise and subverts the cause of the righteous. Justice, and only justice, you shall follow, that you may live and inherit the land that the LORD your God is giving you."

John 7.24; Acts 14.23; Titus 1.5

Deuteronomy 25.1-3

"If there is a dispute between men and they come into court and the judges decide between them, acquitting the innocent and condemning the guilty, then if the guilty man deserves to be beaten, the judge shall cause him to lie down and be beaten in his presence with a number of stripes in proportion to the offense. Forty stripes may be given him, but not more, lest, if one should go on to beat him with more stripes than these, your brother be degraded in your sight."

Deuteronomy 17.8-13

"If any case arises requiring decision between one kind of homicide and another, one kind of legal right and another, or one kind of assault and another, any case within your towns that is too difficult for you, then you shall arise and go up to the place that the LORD your God will choose. And you shall come to the Levitical priests and to the judge who is in office in those days, and you shall consult them, and they shall declare to you the decision. Then you shall do according to what they declare to you from that place that the LORD will choose. And you shall be careful to do according to all that they direct you. According to the instructions that they give you, and according to the decision which they pronounce to you, you shall do. You shall not turn aside from the verdict that they declare to you, either to the right hand or to the left. The man who acts presumptuously by not obeying the priest who stands to minister there before the LORD your God, or the judge, that man shall die. So you shall purge the evil from Israel. And all the people shall hear and fear and not act presumptuously again."

1 Corinthians 16.15, 16; 1 Thessalonians 5.12, 13; Hebrews 13.17

5.4 Civil authorities: Honor God's Law

Civil magistrates must live and rule in accordance with the Law of God.

Deuteronomy 17.14-20

"When you come to the land that the LORD your God is giving you, and you possess it and dwell in it and then say, 'I will set a king over me, like all the nations that are around me,' you may indeed set a king over you whom the LORD your God will choose. One from among your brothers you shall set as king over you. You may not put a foreigner over you, who is not your brother. Only he must not acquire many horses for himself or cause the people to return to Egypt in order to acquire many horses, since the LORD has said to you, 'You shall never return that way again.' And he shall not acquire many wives for himself, lest his heart turn away, nor shall he acquire for himself excessive silver and gold. And when he sits on the throne of his kingdom, he shall write for himself in a book a copy of this law, approved by the Levitical priests. And it shall be with him, and he shall read in it all the days of his life, that he may learn to fear the LORD his God by keeping all the words of this law and these statutes, and doing them, that his heart may not be lifted up above his brothers, and that he may not turn aside from the commandment, either to the right hand or to the left, so that he may continue long in his kingdom, he and his children, in Israel."

2 Samuel 23.3, 4; 1 Kings 6.11-13; Matthew 14.1-4; Acts 23.1-3; Romans 13.1-4; 1 Peter 2.13, 14

5.5 Honor others

We are to show respect to the elderly, the poor, and all other people, because they are the image-bearers of God.

Leviticus 19.32

> "You shall stand up before the gray head and honor the face of an old man, and you shall fear your God: I am the LORD."

Luke 14.7-11; Romans 12.10-17; 1 Peter 2.17

Deuteronomy 24.10-13

> "When you make your neighbor a loan of any sort, you shall not go into his house to collect his pledge. You shall stand outside, and the man to whom you make the loan shall bring the pledge out to you. And if he is a poor man, you shall not sleep in his pledge. You shall restore to him the pledge as the sun sets, that he may sleep in his cloak and bless you. And it shall be righteousness for you before the LORD your God."

5.6 Honor creation

We are to honor the creation, using it in such a way as to conserve it for the future.

Deuteronomy 22.6, 7

> "If you come across a bird's nest in any tree or on the ground, with young ones or eggs and the mother sitting on the young or on the eggs, you shall not take the mother with the young. You shall let the mother go, but the young you may take for yourself, that it may go well with you, and that you may live long."

Genesis 2.15; Psalm 24.1; Psalm 111.2; Romans 8.19-23

Deuteronomy 20.19-20

> "'When you besiege a city for a long time, making war against it in order to take it, you shall not destroy its trees by wielding an axe against them. You may eat from them, but you shall not cut them down. Are the trees in the field human, that they should be besieged by you? Only the trees that you know are not trees for food you may destroy and cut down, that you may build siegeworks against the city that makes war with you, until it falls.'"

6 The Sixth Commandment

You shall not murder

The Commandment

God has made men in His image, and He alone is the Lord of life. We may not unlawfully deprive men of the gift of life; rather, we must do everything in our power to protect and preserve the lives and wellbeing of others.

Exodus 20.13

> "You shall not murder."

Deuteronomy 5.17

> "'You shall not murder.'"

6.1 You shall not hate

We must not allow hate, in any form, to take root in our hearts or come to expression in our lives.

Leviticus 19.17, 18

> "You shall not hate your brother in your heart, but you shall reason frankly with your neighbor, lest you incur sin because of him. You shall not take vengeance or bear a grudge against the sons of your own people, but you shall love your neighbor as yourself: I am the LORD."

Psalm 66.18; Matthew 5.21-24; Luke 6.27, 28; James 4.11, 12; 1 John 2.9-11; 1 John 3.15

6.2 Pay life for life

Retributive justice, including the death penalty, is required to restore righteousness and peace to the community and to quell inclinations to take revenge.

Leviticus 24.17

> "Whoever takes a human life shall surely be put to death."

Leviticus 24.21b

> "...and whoever kills a person shall be put to death."

Deuteronomy 19.11-13

> "'But if anyone hates his neighbor and lies in wait for him and attacks him and strikes him fatally so that he dies, and he flees into one of these cities, then the elders of his city shall send and take him from there, and hand him over to the avenger of blood, so that he may die. Your eye shall not pity him, but you shall purge the guilt of innocent blood from Israel, so that it may be well with you.'"

Numbers 35.16-21

> "But if he struck him down with an iron object, so that he died, he is a murderer. The murderer shall be put to death. And if he struck him down with a stone tool that could cause death, and he died, he is a murderer. The murderer shall be put to death. Or if he struck him down with a wooden tool that could cause death, and he died, he is a murderer. The murderer shall be put to death. The avenger of blood shall himself put the murderer to death; when he meets him, he shall put him to death. And if he pushed him out of hatred or hurled something at him, lying in wait, so that he died, or in enmity struck him down with his hand, so that he died, then he who struck the blow shall be put to death. He is a murderer. The avenger of blood shall put the murderer to death when he meets him."

Exodus 21.12-14

> "Whoever strikes a man so that he dies shall be put to death. But if he did not lie in wait for him, but God let him fall into his hand, then I will appoint for you a place to which he may flee. But if a man willfully attacks another to kill him by cunning, you shall take him from my altar, that he may die."

Exodus 21.22-25

"When men strive together and hit a pregnant woman, so that her children come out, but there is no harm, the one who hit her shall surely be fined, as the woman's husband shall impose on him, and he shall pay as the judges determine. But if there is harm, then you shall pay life for life, eye for eye, tooth for tooth, hand for hand, foot for foot, burn for burn, wound for wound, stripe for stripe."

Deuteronomy 22.25-27

"But if in the open country a man meets a young woman who is betrothed, and the man seizes her and lies with her, then only the man who lay with her shall die. But you shall do nothing to the young woman; she has committed no offense punishable by death. For this case is like that of a man attacking and murdering his neighbor, because he met her in the open country, and though the betrothed young woman cried for help there was no one to rescue her."

Matthew 5.38-48

Leviticus 24.17-23

"Whoever takes a human life shall surely be put to death. Whoever takes an animal's life shall make it good, life for life. If anyone injures his neighbor, as he has done it shall be done to him, fracture for fracture, eye for eye, tooth for tooth; whatever injury he has given a person shall be given to him. Whoever kills an animal shall make it good, and whoever kills a person shall be put to death. You shall have the same rule for the sojourner and for the native, for I am the LORD your God." So Moses spoke to the people of Israel, and they brought out of the camp the one who had cursed and stoned him with stones. Thus the people of Israel did as the LORD commanded Moses.

Deuteronomy 24.16

"'Fathers shall not be put to death because of their children, nor shall children be put to death because of their fathers. Each one shall be put to death for his own sin.'"

Exodus 21.28-31

> "When an ox gores a man or a woman to death, the ox shall be stoned, and its flesh shall not be eaten, but the owner of the ox shall not be liable. But if the ox has been accustomed to gore in the past, and its owner has been warned but has not kept it in, and it kills a man or a woman, the ox shall be stoned, and its owner also shall be put to death. If a ransom is imposed on him, then he shall give for the redemption of his life whatever is imposed on him. If it gores a man's son or daughter, he shall be dealt with according to this same rule. If the ox gores a slave, male or female, the owner shall give to their master thirty shekels of silver, and the ox shall be stoned."

6.3 Protect the lives of others

Human life is valuable because it bears the image of God. We must guard against any eruption of affection or error of judgment that might bring unjust harm to others or jeopardize their lives.

Deuteronomy 19.1-10

> "'When the LORD your God cuts off the nations whose land the LORD your God is giving you, and you dispossess them and dwell in their cities and in their houses, you shall set apart three cities for yourselves in the land that the LORD your God is giving you to possess. ³You shall measure the distances and divide into three parts the area of the land that the LORD your God gives you as a possession, so that any manslayer can flee to them. ⁴'This is the provision for the manslayer, who by fleeing there may save his life. If anyone kills his neighbor unintentionally without having hated him in the past-- as when someone goes into the forest with his neighbor to cut wood, and his hand swings the axe to cut down a tree, and the head slips from the handle and strikes his neighbor so that he dies--he may flee to one of these cities and live, ⁶lest the avenger of blood in hot anger pursue the manslayer and overtake him, because the way is long, and strike him fatally, though the man did not deserve to die, since he had not hated his neighbor in the past. ⁷Therefore I command you, You shall set apart three cities. ⁸And if the LORD your God enlarges your territory, as he has sworn to your fathers, and gives you all the land that he promised to give to your fathers-- ⁹provided you are careful to keep all this commandment, which I command you today, by loving the LORD your God and by walking ever in his ways--then you shall add three other cities to these three, lest innocent blood be shed in your land that the LORD

your God is giving you for an inheritance, and so the guilt of bloodshed be upon you.'"

Numbers 35:22-29

"But if he pushed him suddenly without enmity, or hurled anything on him without lying in wait or used a stone that could cause death, and without seeing him dropped it on him, so that he died, though he was not his enemy and did not seek his harm, then the congregation shall judge between the manslayer and the avenger of blood, in accordance with these rules. And the congregation shall rescue the manslayer from the hand of the avenger of blood, and the congregation shall restore him to his city of refuge to which he had fled, and he shall live in it until the death of the high priest who was anointed with the holy oil. But if the manslayer shall at any time go beyond the boundaries of his city of refuge to which he fled, and the avenger of blood finds him outside the boundaries of his city of refuge, and the avenger of blood kills the manslayer, he shall not be guilty of blood. For he must remain in his city of refuge until the death of the high priest, but after the death of the high priest the manslayer may return to the land of his possession. And these things shall be for a statute and rule for you throughout your generations in all your dwelling places."

Numbers 35.9-15

And the LORD spoke to Moses, saying, "Speak to the people of Israel and say to them, When you cross the Jordan into the land of Canaan, then you shall select cities to be cities of refuge for you, that the manslayer who kills any person without intent may flee there. The cities shall be for you a refuge from the avenger, that the manslayer may not die until he stands before the congregation for judgment. And the cities that you give shall be your six cities of refuge. You shall give three cities beyond the Jordan, and three cities in the land of Canaan, to be cities of refuge. These six cities shall be for refuge for the people of Israel, and for the stranger and for the sojourner among them, that anyone who kills any person without intent may flee there."

Exodus 21.20, 21

"When a man strikes his slave, male or female, with a rod and the slave dies under his hand, he shall be avenged. But if the slave survives a day or two, he is not to be avenged, for the slave is his money."

Deuteronomy 24.6

> "No one shall take a mill or an upper millstone in pledge, for that would be taking a life in pledge."

Deuteronomy 22.8

> "When you build a new house, you shall make a parapet for your roof, that you may not bring the guilt of blood upon your house, if anyone should fall from it."

1 Corinthians 8.9-12

Deuteronomy 25.11, 12

> "When men fight with one another and the wife of the one draws near to rescue her husband from the hand of him who is beating him and puts out her hand and seizes him by the private parts, then you shall cut off her hand. Your eye shall have no pity."

7   The Seventh Commandment

You shall not commit adultery

The Commandment

This commandment forbids all unlawful sexual practices and relations, that is, those engaged outside the bounds of marriage.

Exodus 20.14

> "You shall not commit adultery."

Deuteronomy 5.18

> "'And you shall not commit adultery.'"

Ephesians 5.3-13; 1 Thessalonians 4.3-8

7.1 Do not uncover nakedness

These statutes forbid looking upon the unclothed bodies of others with sexual desire.

Leviticus 18.6-18

> "None of you shall approach any one of his close relatives to uncover nakedness. I am the LORD. You shall not uncover the nakedness of your father, which is the nakedness of your mother; she is your mother, you shall not uncover her nakedness. You shall not uncover the nakedness of your father's wife; it is your father's nakedness. You shall not uncover the nakedness of your sister, your father's daughter or your mother's daughter, whether brought up in the family or in another home. You shall not uncover the nakedness of your son's daughter or of your daughter's daughter, for their nakedness is your own nakedness. You shall not uncover the nakedness of your father's wife's daughter, brought up in your father's family, since she is your sister. You shall not uncover the nakedness of your father's sister; she is your father's relative. You shall not uncover the nakedness of your mother's sister, for she is your mother's relative. You shall not uncover the nakedness of your father's brother, that is, you shall not approach his wife; she is your aunt. You shall not uncover the nakedness of your daughter-in-law; she is your son's wife, you shall not

uncover her nakedness. You shall not uncover the nakedness of your brother's wife; it is your brother's nakedness. You shall not uncover the nakedness of a woman and of her daughter, and you shall not take her son's daughter or her daughter's daughter to uncover her nakedness; they are relatives; it is depravity. And you shall not take a woman as a rival wife to her sister, uncovering her nakedness while her sister is still alive."

Matthew 5.27, 28

Leviticus 20.17

"If a man takes his sister, a daughter of his father or a daughter of his mother, and sees her nakedness, and she sees his nakedness, it is a disgrace, and they shall be cut off in the sight of the children of their people. He has uncovered his sister's nakedness, and he shall bear his iniquity."

Leviticus 18.19

"You shall not approach a woman to uncover her nakedness while she is in her menstrual uncleanness."

Leviticus 20.18

"If a man lies with a woman during her menstrual period and uncovers her nakedness, he has made naked her fountain, and she has uncovered the fountain of her blood. Both of them shall be cut off from among their people."

Leviticus 20.19

"You shall not uncover the nakedness of your mother's sister or of your father's sister, for that is to make naked one's relative; they shall bear their iniquity."

Leviticus 20.21

"If a man takes his brother's wife, it is impurity. He has uncovered his brother's nakedness; they shall be childless."

7.2 Do not commit unlawful relations between men and women

Adultery in all its forms is condemned.

Leviticus 18.20

"And you shall not lie sexually with your neighbor's wife and so make yourself unclean with her."

1 Corinthians 10.8

Leviticus 20.10

"If a man commits adultery with the wife of his neighbor, both the adulterer and the adulteress shall surely be put to death."

Deuteronomy 22.22

"If a man is found lying with the wife of another man, both of them shall die, the man who lay with the woman, and the woman. So you shall purge the evil from Israel."

Deuteronomy 22.30

"A man shall not take his father's wife, so that he does not uncover his father's nakedness."

1 Corinthians 5.1, 2, 13

Leviticus 20.11

"If a man lies with his father's wife, he has uncovered his father's nakedness; both of them shall surely be put to death; their blood is upon them."

1 Corinthians 5.1, 2, 13

Leviticus 20.20

"If a man lies with his uncle's wife, he has uncovered his uncle's nakedness; they shall bear their sin; they shall die childless."

Leviticus 20.12

> "If a man lies with his daughter-in-law, both of them shall surely be put to death; they have committed perversion; their blood is upon them."

7.3 Do not commit other unlawful relations

Do not allow those practices that cheapen sexuality and threaten the integrity and lawful purposes of sexual activity.

Leviticus 20.14

> "If a man takes a woman and her mother also, it is depravity; he and they shall be burned with fire, that there may be no depravity among you."

Exodus 22.16, 17

> "If a man seduces a virgin who is not engaged to be married and lies with her, he shall give the bride-price for her and make her his wife. If her father utterly refuses to give her to him, he shall pay money equal to the bride-price for virgins."

Deuteronomy 22.28, 29

> "If a man meets a virgin who is not betrothed, and seizes her and lies with her, and they are found, then the man who lay with her shall give to the father of the young woman fifty shekels of silver, and she shall be his wife, because he has violated her. He may not divorce her all his days."

Deuteronomy 22.23, 24

> "If there is a betrothed virgin, and a man meets her in the city and lies with her, then you shall bring them both out to the gate of that city, and you shall stone them to death with stones, the young woman because she did not cry for help though she was in the city, and the man because he violated his neighbor's wife. So you shall purge the evil from your midst."

Deuteronomy 22.25-27

> "But if in the open country a man meets a young woman who is betrothed, and the man seizes her and lies with her, then only the man who lay with her shall die. But you shall do nothing to the young woman; she has committed no offense punishable by death. For this case is like that of a

man attacking and murdering his neighbor, because he met her in the open country, and though the betrothed young woman cried for help there was none to rescue her."

Leviticus 19.29

"Do not profane your daughter by making her a prostitute, lest the land fall into prostitution and the land become full of depravity."

Leviticus 18.22

"You shall not lie with a male as with a woman; it is an abomination."

Leviticus 20.13

"If a man lies with a male as with a woman, both of them have committed an abomination; they shall surely be put to death; their blood is upon them."

Leviticus 18.23

"And you shall not lie with any animal and so make yourself unclean with it, neither shall any woman give herself to an animal to lie with it: it is perversion."

Exodus 22.19

"Whoever lies with an animal shall be put to death."

Leviticus 20.15, 16

"If a man lies with an animal, he shall surely be put to death, and you shall kill the animal. If a woman approaches any animal and lies with it, you shall kill the woman and the animal; they shall surely be put to death; their blood is upon them."

7.4 Regulate divorce

Divorce is permitted under certain conditions of indecency.

Deuteronomy 24.1-4

> "'When a man takes a wife and marries her, if then she finds no favor in his eyes because he has found some indecency in her, and he writes her a certificate of divorce and puts it in her hand and sends her out of his house, and she departs out of his house, and if she goes and becomes another man's wife, and the latter man hates her and writes her a certificate of divorce and puts it in her hand and sends her out of his house, or if the latter man dies, who took her to be his wife, then her former husband, who sent her away, may not take her again to be his wife, after she has been defiled, for that is an abomination before the LORD. And you shall not bring sin upon the land that the LORD your God is giving you for an inheritance.'"

8   The Eighth Commandment

You shall not steal

The Commandment

God is sovereign in the disposition of blessings, and He calls each of us to exercise proper stewardship over what He has entrusted to us, and to respect and preserve the stewardship of others. We must not, by stealing in any way, violate the divine economy and the stewardship rights and duties of others.

Exodus 20.15

> "You shall not steal."

Deuteronomy 5.19

> "'And you shall not steal.'"

8.1 Guard against negligence

Love for neighbor requires active concern for their property and full restoration of any loss we may cause.

Exodus 22.6

> "If fire breaks out and catches in thorns so that the stacked grain or the standing grain or the field is consumed, he who started the fire shall make full restitution."

James 3.5, 6

Exodus 22.5

> "If a man causes a field or vineyard to be grazed over, or lets his beast loose and it feeds in another man's field, he shall make restitution from the best in his own field and in his own vineyard."

Deuteronomy 22.1-4

> "'You shall not see your brother's ox or his sheep going astray and ignore them. You shall take them back to your brother. And if he does not live near you and you do not know who he is, you shall bring it home to your house, and it shall stay with you until your brother seeks it. Then you shall restore it to him. And you shall do the same with his donkey or with his garment, or with any lost thing of your brother's, which he loses and you find; you may not ignore it. You shall not see your brother's donkey or his ox fallen down by the way and ignore them. You shall help him to lift them up again.'"

Exodus 21.33, 34

> "When a man opens a pit, or when a man digs a pit and does not cover it, and an ox or a donkey falls into it, the owner of the pit shall make restoration. He shall give money to its owner, and the dead beast shall be his."

Exodus 21.35, 36

> "When one man's ox butts another's, so that it dies, then they shall sell the live ox and share its price, and the dead beast also they shall share. Or if it is known that the ox has been accustomed to gore in the past, and its owner has not kept it in, he shall repay ox for ox, and the dead beast shall be his."

8.2 Do not withhold what is due

God's people are to be actively concerned to preserve the property and wellbeing of their neighbors, and to ensure that each receives what he is due.

Numbers 27.8-11

> "And you shall speak to the people of Israel, saying, 'If a man dies and has no son, then you shall transfer his inheritance to his daughter. And if he has no daughter, then you shall give his inheritance to his brothers. And if he has no brothers, then you shall give his inheritance to his father's brothers. And if his father has not brothers, then you shall give his inheritance to the nearest kinsman of his clan, and he shall possess it. And it shall be for the people of Israel a statute and a rule, as the LORD commanded Moses.'"

Ruth 4

Deuteronomy 25.5-10

> "'If brothers dwell together, and one of them dies and has no son, the wife of the dead man shall not be married outside the family to a stranger. Her husband's brother shall go in to her and take her as his wife and perform the duty of a husband's brother to her. And the first son whom she bears shall succeed to the name of his dead brother, that his name may not be blotted out of Israel. And if the man does not wish to take his brother's wife, then his brother's wife shall go up to the gate to the elders and say, "My husband's brother refuses to perpetuate his brother's name in Israel; he will not perform the duty of a husband's brother to me." Then the elders of his city shall call him and speak to him, and if he persists, saying, "I do not wish to take her," then his brother's wife shall go up to him in the presence of the elders and pull his sandal off his foot and spit in his face. And she shall answer and say, "So shall it be done to the man who does not build up his brother's house." And the name of his house shall be called in Israel, "The house of him who had his sandal pulled off.'"'

Ruth 4

Exodus 21.18, 19

> "When men quarrel and one strikes the other with a stone or with his fist and the man does not die but takes to his bed, then if the man rises again and walks outdoors with his staff, he who struck him shall be clear; only he shall pay for the loss of his time, and shall have him thoroughly healed."

Luke 10.25-37

Exodus 22.7, 8

> "If a man gives to his neighbor money or goods to keep safe, and it is stolen from the man's house, then, if the thief is found, he shall pay double. If the thief is not found, the owner of the house shall come near to God to show whether or not he has put his hand to his neighbor's property."

Exodus 22.14, 15

"If a man borrows anything of his neighbor, and it is injured or dies, the owner not being with it, he shall make full restitution. If the owner was with it, he shall not make restitution; if it was hired, it came for its hiring fee."

Deuteronomy 23.19, 20

"'You shall not charge interest on loans to your brother, interest on money, interest on food, interest on anything that is lent for interest. You may charge a foreigner interest, but you may not charge your brother interest, that the LORD your God may bless you in all that you undertake in the land that you are entering to take possession of it.'"

Exodus 22.25; Leviticus 25.1-7, 8-22, 35-38; Deuteronomy 15.1-6, 9, 10

Exodus 22.26, 27

"If ever you take your neighbor's cloak in pledge, you shall return it to him before the sun goes down, for that is his only covering, and it is his cloak for his body; in what else shall he sleep? And if he cries to me, I will hear, for I am compassionate."

Leviticus 19.13

"You shall not oppress your neighbor or rob him. The wages of a hired servant shall not remain with you all night until the morning."

Deuteronomy 24.14, 15

"'You shall not oppress a hired servant who is poor and needy, whether he is one of your brothers or one of the sojourners who are in your land within your towns. You shall give him his wages on the same day, before the sun sets (for he is poor and counts on it), lest he cry against you to the LORD, and you be guilty of sin.'"

James 5.1-4

Deuteronomy 12.19

"'Take care that you do not neglect the Levite as long as you live in your land.'"

Deuteronomy 14.27

> "'And you shall not neglect the Levite who is within your towns, for he has no portion or inheritance with you.'"

1 Corinthians 9.3-14

Exodus 22.9

> "For every breach of trust, whether it is for an ox, for a donkey, for a sheep, for a cloak, or for any kind of lost thing, of which one says, 'This is it,' the case of both parties shall come before God. The one whom God condemns shall pay double to his neighbor."

Exodus 22.10-13

> "If a man gives to his neighbor a donkey or an ox or a sheep or any beast to keep safe, and it dies or is injured or is driven away, without anyone seeing it, an oath by the LORD shall be between them both to see whether or not he has put his hand to his neighbor's property. The owner shall accept the oath, and he shall not make restitution. But if it is stolen from him, he shall make restitution to its owner. If it is torn by beasts, let him bring it as evidence. He shall not make restitution for what has been torn."

Deuteronomy 25.4

> "'You shall not muzzle an ox when it is treading out the grain.'"

Matthew 10.10; Luke 10.7; 1 Corinthians 9.8-12

8.3 Preserve personal property

These statutes provide for restitution of stolen property and direct us to love even our enemies by caring for their property.

Leviticus 19.13

> "You shall not oppress your neighbor or rob him."

Exodus 22.2, 3

> "If a thief is found breaking in and is struck so that he dies, there shall be no bloodguilt for him, but if the sun has risen on him, there shall be

bloodguilt for him. He shall surely pay. If he has nothing, then he shall be sold for his theft."

Exodus 22.4

"If the stolen beast is found alive in his possession, whether it is an ox or a donkey or a sheep, he shall pay double."

Exodus 22.1

"If a man steals an ox or a sheep, and kills it or sells it, he shall repay five oxen for an ox, and four sheep for a sheep."

Luke 19.1-9

Leviticus 24.21a

"Whoever kills an animal shall make it good…"

Leviticus 24.18

"Whoever takes an animal's life shall make it good, life for life."

Deuteronomy 23.24, 25

"'If you go into your neighbor's vineyard, you may eat your fill of grapes, as many as you wish, but you shall not put any in your bag. If you go into your neighbor's standing grain, you may pluck the ears with your hand, but you shall not put a sickle to your neighbor's standing grain.'"

Exodus 23.4, 5

"If you meet your enemy's ox or his donkey going astray, you shall bring it back to him. If you see the donkey of one who hates you lying down under its burden, you shall refrain from leaving him with it; you shall rescue it with him."

Matthew 5.38-42; Romans 12.21

8.4 Punish kidnappers

No one has the right to deprive another of his liberty in an unlawful manner.

Exodus 21.16

"Whoever steals a man and sells him, and anyone found in possession of him, shall be put to death."

Deuteronomy 24.7

"'If a man is found stealing one of his brothers, of the people of Israel, and if he treats him as a slave or sells him, then that thief shall die. So you shall purge the evil from your midst.'"

8.5 Do justice to the poor, the sojourners, and the needy

Do not neglect, and do not take advantage of, the poor and needy; rather, make it possible for them to know justice and provision with dignity.

Deuteronomy 15.11

"'For there will never cease to be poor in the land. Therefore I command you, "You shall open wide your hand to your brother, to the needy and to the poor, in your land."'"

Psalm 41.1; Galatians 2.10

Deuteronomy 15.7, 8

"'If among you, one of your brothers should become poor, in any of your towns within your land that the LORD your God is giving you, you shall not harden your heart or shut your hand against your poor brother, but you shall open your hand to him and lend him sufficient for his need, whatever it may be.'"

Deuteronomy 24.17, 18

"'You shall not pervert the justice due to the sojourner or to the fatherless, or take a widow's garment in pledge, but you shall remember that you were a slave in Egypt and the LORD your God redeemed you from there; therefore I command you to do this.'"

Deuteronomy 10.18, 19; Malachi 3.5

Exodus 22.21-24

> "You shall not wrong a sojourner or oppress him, for you were sojourners
> in the land of Egypt. You shall not mistreat any widow or fatherless child.
> If you do mistreat them, and they cry out to me, I will surely hear their cry,
> and my wrath will burn, and I will kill you with the sword, and your wives
> shall become widows and your children fatherless."

Exodus 22.25

> "If you lend money to any of my people with you who is poor, you shall
> not be like a moneylender to him, and you shall not exact interest from
> him."

Deuteronomy 23.19, 20

Leviticus 19.33, 34

> "When a stranger sojourns with you in your land, you shall not do him
> wrong. You shall treat the stranger who sojourns with you as the native
> among you, and you shall love him as yourself, for you were strangers in
> the land of Egypt: I am the LORD your God."

Deuteronomy 10.17-19

Exodus 23.9

> "You shall not oppress a sojourner. You know the heart of a sojourner, for
> you were sojourners in the land of Egypt."

Exodus 23.6-8

> "You shall not pervert the justice due to your poor in his lawsuit. [7]Keep far
> from a false charge, and do not kill the innocent and righteous, for I will
> not acquit the wicked. And you shall take no bribe, for a bribe blinds the
> clear-sighted and subverts the cause of those who are in the right."

Leviticus 25.35-38

> "If your brother becomes poor and cannot maintain himself with you, you
> shall support him as though he were a stranger and a sojourner, and he

shall live with you. Take no interest from him or profit, but fear your God, that your brother may live beside you. You shall not lend him your money at interest, nor give him your food for profit. I am the LORD your God, who brought you out of the land of Egypt to give you the land of Canaan, and to be your God."

Leviticus 25.39-43

"If your brother becomes poor beside you and sells himself to you, you shall not make him serve as a slave: he shall be with you as a hired servant and as a sojourner. He shall serve with you until the year of the jubilee. Then he shall go out from you, he and his children with him, and go back to his own clan and return to the possession of his fathers. For they are my servants, whom I brought out of the land of Egypt; they shall not be sold as slaves. You shall not rule over him ruthlessly but shall fear your God."

Leviticus 19.14

"You shall not curse the deaf or put a stumbling block before the blind, but you shall fear your God: I am the LORD."

Deuteronomy 15.9-10

"'Take care lest there be an unworthy thought in your heart and you say, "The seventh year, the year of release is near," and your eye look grudgingly on your poor brother, and you give him nothing, and he cry to the LORD against you, and you be guilty of sin. You shall give to him freely, and your heart shall not be grudging when you give to him, because for this the LORD your God will bless you in all your work and in all that you undertake.'"

Leviticus 23.22

"And when you reap the harvest of your land, you shall not reap your field right up to its edge, nor shall you gather the gleanings after your harvest. You shall leave them for the poor and for the sojourner: I am the LORD your God."

2 Thessalonians 3.10

Leviticus 19.9, 10

"When you reap the harvest of your land, you shall not reap your field right up to its edge, neither shall you gather the gleanings after your harvest. And you shall not strip your vineyard bare, neither shall you gather the fallen grapes of your vineyard. You shall leave them for the poor and for the sojourner: I am the LORD your God."

2 Thessalonians 3.10

Deuteronomy 24.19-22

"'When you reap your harvest in your field and forget a sheaf in the field, you shall not go back to get it. It shall be for the sojourner, the fatherless, and the widow, that the LORD your God may bless you in all the work of your hands. When you beat your olive trees, you shall not go over them again. It shall be for the sojourner, the fatherless, and the widow. When you gather the grapes of your vineyard, you shall not strip it afterward. It shall be for the sojourner, the fatherless, and the widow. You shall remember that you were a slave in the land of Egypt; therefore I command you to do this.'"

Deuteronomy 14.28, 29

"'At the end of every three years you shall bring out all the tithe of your produce in the same year and lay it up within your towns. And the Levite, because he has no portion or inheritance with you, and the sojourner, the fatherless, and the widow, who are within your towns, shall come and eat and be filled, that the LORD your God may bless you in all the work of your hands that you do.'"

Exodus 23.10, 11

"For six years you shall sow your land and gather in its yield, but the seventh year you shall let it rest and lie fallow, that the poor of your people may eat; and what they leave the beasts of the field may eat. You shall do likewise with your vineyard, and with your olive orchard."

8.6 Regulate slavery

Slavery was allowed in ancient Israel, but only within strict parameters of justice and fairness for the enslaved.

Leviticus 25.44-46

"As for your male and female slaves whom you may have: you may buy male and female slaves from among the nations that are around you. You may also buy from among the strangers who sojourn with you and their clans that are with you, who have been born in your land, and they may be your property. You may bequeath them to your sons after you to inherit as a possession forever. You may make slaves of them, but over your brothers the people of Israel you shall not rule, one over another ruthlessly."

Exodus 21.2-6

"When you buy a Hebrew slave, he shall serve six years, and in the seventh he shall go out free, for nothing. If he comes in single, he shall go out single; if he comes in married, then his wife shall go out with him. If his master gives him a wife and she bears him sons or daughters, the wife and her children shall be her master's, and he shall go out alone. But if the slave plainly says, 'I love my master, my wife, and my children; I will not go out free,' then his master shall bring him to God, and he shall bring him to the door or the doorpost. And his master shall bore his ear through with an awl, and he shall be his slave forever."

Deuteronomy 15.12-18

"'If your brother, a Hebrew man or a Hebrew woman, is sold to you, he shall serve you six years, and in the seventh year you shall let him go free from you. And when you let him go free from you, you shall not let him go empty-handed. You shall furnish him liberally out of your flock, out of your threshing floor, and out of your winepress. As the LORD your God has blessed you, you shall give to him. You shall remember that you were a slave in the land of Egypt, and the LORD your God redeemed you; therefore I command you this today. But if he says to you, "I will not go out from you," because he loves you and your household, since he is well-off with you, then you shall take an awl, and put it through his ear into the door, and he shall be your slave forever. And to your female slave you shall do the same. It shall not seem hard to you when you let him go free from you, for at half the cost of a hired servant he has served you six years. So the LORD your God will bless you in all that you do.'"

Exodus 21.7-11

"When a man sells his daughter as a slave, she shall not go out as the male slaves do. If she does not please her master, who has designated her for himself, then he shall let her be redeemed. He shall have no right to sell her to a foreign people, since he has broken faith with her. If he designates her for his son, he shall deal with her as with a daughter. If he takes another wife to himself, he shall not diminish her food, her clothing, or her marital rights. And if he does not do these three things for her, she shall go out for nothing, without payment of money."

Exodus 21.26, 27

"When a man strikes the eye of his slave, male or female, and destroys it, he shall let the slave go free because of his eye. If he knocks out the tooth of his slave, male or female, he shall let the slave go free because of his tooth."

Leviticus 25.47-55

"If a stranger or sojourner with you becomes rich, and your brother beside him becomes poor and sells himself to the stranger or sojourner with you or to a member of the stranger's clan, then after he is sold he may be redeemed. One of his brothers may redeem him, or his uncle or his cousin may redeem him, or a close relative from his clan may redeem him. Or if he grows rich he may redeem himself. He shall calculate with his buyer from the year when he sold himself to him until the year of jubilee, and the price of his sale shall vary with the number of years. The time he was with his owner shall be rated as the time of a hired servant. If there are still many years left, he shall pay proportionately for his redemption some of his sale price. If there remain but a few years until the year of jubilee, he shall calculate and pay for his redemption in proportion to his years of service. He shall treat him as a servant hired year by year. He shall not rule ruthlessly over him in your sight. And if he is not redeemed by these means, then he and his children with him shall be released in the year of jubilee. For it is to me that the people of Israel are servants. They are my servants whom I brought out of the land of Egypt: I am the LORD your God."

Deuteronomy 23.15-16

> "'You shall not give up to his master a slave who has escaped from his master to you. He shall dwell with you, in your midst, in the place that he shall choose within one of your towns, wherever it suits him. You shall not wrong him.'"

Philemon 8-16

8.7 Do justice in time of war

Wage war when necessary without fear and in order to secure the promises of God.

Deuteronomy 24.5

> "'When a man is newly married, he shall not go out with the army or be liable for any other public duty. He shall be free at home one year to be happy with his wife whom he has taken.'"

Deuteronomy 20.1-9

> "'When you go out to war against your enemies, and see horses and chariots and an army larger than your own, you shall not be afraid of them, for the LORD your God is with you, who brought you up out of the land of Egypt. And when you draw near to the battle, the priest shall come forward and speak to the people and shall say to them, "Hear, O Israel, today you are drawing near for battle against your enemies: let not your heart faint. Do not fear or panic or be in dread of them, for the LORD your God is he who goes with you to fight for you against your enemies, to give you the victory." Then the officers shall speak to the people, saying, "Is there any man who has built a new house and has not dedicated it? Let him go back to his house, lest he die in the battle and another man dedicate it. And is there any man who has planted a vineyard and has not enjoyed its fruit? Let him go back to his house, lest he die in the battle and another man enjoy its fruit. And is there any man who has betrothed a wife and has not taken her? Let him go back to his house, lest he die in the battle and another man take her." And the officers shall speak further to the people, and say, "Is there any man who is fearful and fainthearted? Let him go back to his house, lest he make the heart of his fellows melt like his own." And when the officers have finished speaking to the people, then commanders shall be appointed at the head of the people.'"

Deuteronomy 20.10-18

"'When you draw near to a city to fight against it, offer terms of peace to it. And if it responds to you peaceably and it opens to you, then all the people who are found in it shall do forced labor for you and shall serve you. But if it makes no peace with you, but makes war against you, then you shall besiege it. And when the LORD your God gives it into your hand, you shall put all its males to the sword, but the women and the little ones, the livestock, and everything else in the city, all its spoil, you shall take as plunder for yourselves. And you shall enjoy the spoil of your enemies, which the LORD your God has given you. Thus you shall do to all the cities that are very far from you, which are not cities of the nations here. But in the cities of these peoples that the LORD your God is giving you for an inheritance, you shall save alive nothing that breathes, but you shall devote them to complete destruction, the Hittites and the Amorites, the Canaanites and the Perizzites, the Hivites and the Jebusites, as the LORD your God has commanded, that they may not teach you to do according to all their abominable practices that they have done for their gods, and so you sin against the LORD your God.'"

9   The Ninth Commandment

You shall not bear false witness

The Commandment

God is a God of Truth, and He has entrusted to us a stewardship of His Truth, such that we must always be diligent to speak the truth in love, and to deal truthfully with God and with our neighbor.

Exodus 20.16

> "You shall not bear false witness against your neighbor."

Deuteronomy 5.20

> "'And you shall not bear false witness against your neighbor.'"

9.1 Be truthful to God

We are to be holy to the Lord in all things and diligent to fulfill our vows.

Deuteronomy 6.16-19

> [16]"'You shall not put the LORD your God to the test, as you tested him at Massah. You shall diligently keep the commandments of the LORD your God, and his testimonies and his statutes, which he has commanded you. And you shall do what is right and good in the sight of the LORD, that it may go well with you, and that you may go in and take possession of the good land that the LORD swore to give to your fathers by thrusting out all your enemies from before you, as the LORD has promised.'"

Leviticus 18.24-30

> "Do not make yourselves unclean by any of these things, for by all these the nations I am driving out before you have become unclean, and the land became unclean, so that I punished its iniquity, and the land vomited out its inhabitants. But you shall keep my statutes and my rules and do none of these abominations, either the native or the stranger who sojourns among you (for the people of the land, who were before you, did all of these abominations, so that the land became unclean), lest the land vomit you out when you make it unclean, as it vomited out the nation that was before

you. For everyone who does any of these abominations, the persons who do them shall be cut off from among their people. So keep my charge never to practice any of these abominable customs that were practiced before you, and never to make yourselves unclean by them: I am the LORD your God."

Deuteronomy 23.21-23

"'If you make a vow to the LORD your God, you shall not delay fulfilling it, for the LORD your God will surely require it of you, and you will be guilty of sin. But if you refrain from vowing, you will not be guilty of sin. You shall be careful to do what has passed your lips, for you have voluntarily vowed to the LORD your God what you have promised with your mouth.'"

Ecclesiastes 5.4-6

9.2 *Be truthful to your neighbor*

Do not lie to, deceive, or otherwise deal falsely or dishonestly with your neighbor.

Leviticus 19.11

"You shall not steal; you shall not deal falsely; you shall not lie to one another."

Colossians 3.9

Leviticus 6.1-5

The LORD spoke to Moses, saying, "If anyone sins and commits a breach of faith against the LORD by deceiving his neighbor in a matter of deposit or security, or through robbery, or if he has oppressed his neighbor or has found something lost and lied about it, swearing falsely – in any of all the things that people do and sin thereby – if he has sinned and has realized his guilt and will restore what he took by robbery or what he got by oppression or the deposit that was committed to him or the lost thing that he found or anything about which he has sworn falsely, he shall restore it in full and shall add a fifth to it, and give it to him to whom it belongs on the day he realizes his guilt."

Leviticus 5.4, 5

…or if anyone utters with his lips a rash oath to do evil or to do good, any sort of rash oath that people swear, and it is hidden from him, when he comes to know it, and he realizes his guilt in any of these; when he realizes his guilt in any of these and confesses the sin he has committed…

Deuteronomy 25.13-16

"'You shall not have in your bag two kinds of weights, a large and a small. You shall not have in your house two kinds of measures, a large and a small. A full and fair weight you shall have, a full and fair measure you shall have, that your days may be long in the land that the LORD your God is giving you. For all who do such things, all who act dishonestly, are an abomination to the LORD your God.'"

Deuteronomy 22.13-21

"'If any man takes a wife and goes in to her and then hates her and accuses her of misconduct and brings a bad name upon her, saying, "I took this woman, and when I came near her, I did not find in her evidence of virginity," then the father of the young woman and her mother shall take and bring out the evidence of her virginity to the elders of the city in the gate. And the father of the young woman shall say to the elders, "I gave my daughter to this man to marry, and he hates her; and behold, he has accused her of misconduct, saying, 'I did not find in your daughter evidence of virginity.' And yet this is the evidence of my daughter's virginity." And they shall spread the cloak before the elders of the city. Then the elders of that city shall take the man and whip him, and they shall fine him a hundred shekels of silver and give them to the father of the young woman, because he has brought a bad name upon a virgin of Israel. And she shall be his wife. He may not divorce her all his days. But if the thing is true, that evidence of virginity was not found in the young woman, then they shall bring out the young woman to the door of her father's house, and the men of her city shall stone her to death with stones, because she has done an outrageous thing in Israel by whoring in her father's house. So you shall purge the evil from your midst.'"

Deuteronomy 22.5

"'A woman shall not wear a man's garment, nor shall a man put on a woman's cloak, for whoever does these things is an abomination to the LORD your God.'"

9.3 Do not conspire falsely

Do not join with others to spread false reports or to bring false charges.

Exodus 23.1

"You shall not spread a false report. You shall not join hands with a wicked man to be a malicious witness."

Exodus 23.2, 3

"You shall not fall in with the many to do evil, nor shall you bear witness in a lawsuit, siding with the many, so as to pervert justice, nor shall you be partial to a poor man in his lawsuit."

9.4 Do justice at law

Be sure to be truthful, honest, and fair in all matters of legal judgment.

Leviticus 19.15, 16

"You shall do no injustice in court. You shall not be partial to the poor or defer to the great, but in righteousness shall you judge your neighbor. You shall not go around as a slanderer among your people, and you shall not stand up against the life of your neighbor: I am the LORD."

John 7.24

Leviticus 19.35

"You shall do no wrong in judgment, in measures of length or weight or quantity."

Leviticus 19.35, 36

"You shall do no wrong in judgment, in measures of length or weight or quantity. You shall have just balances, just weights, a just ephah, and a just hin: I am the LORD your God, who brought you out of the land of Egypt."

Deuteronomy 19.15-21

> "'A single witness shall not suffice against a person for any crime or for
> any wrong in connection with any offense that he has committed. Only on
> the evidence of two witnesses or of three witnesses shall a charge be
> established. If a malicious witness arises to accuse a person of wrongdoing,
> then both parties to the dispute shall appear before the LORD, before the
> priests and the judges who are in office in those days. The judges shall
> inquire diligently, and if the witness is a false witness and has accused his
> brother falsely, then you shall do to him as he had meant to do to his
> brother. So you shall purge the evil from your midst. And the rest shall
> hear and fear, and shall never again commit any such evil among you. Your
> eye shall not pity. It shall be life for life, eye for eye, tooth for tooth, hand
> for hand, foot for foot.'"

Numbers 35:30-34

> "If anyone kills a person, the murderer shall be put to death on the
> evidence of witnesses. But no person shall be put to death on the
> testimony of one witness. Moreover, you shall accept no ransom for the
> life of a murderer, who is guilty of death, but he shall be put to death. And
> you shall accept no ransom for him who has fled to his city of refuge, that
> he may return to dwell in the land before the death of the high priest. You
> shall not pollute the land in which you live, for blood pollutes the land, and
> no atonement can be made for the land for the blood that is shed in it,
> except by the blood of the one who shed it. You shall not defile the land in
> which you live, in the midst of which I dwell, for I the LORD dwell in the
> midst of the people of Israel."

Leviticus 5.1

> "If anyone sins in that he hears a public adjuration to testify, and though
> he is a witness, whether he has seen or come to know the matter, yet does
> not speak, he shall bear his iniquity…"

10   The Tenth Commandment

You shall not covet

The Commandment

Covetousness is unlawful desire, and is a gateway to all other sin. We must guard against covetousness and not allow it any place in our hearts.

Exodus 20.17

> "You shall not covet your neighbor's house; you shall not covet your neighbor's wife, or his male servant, or his female servant, or his ox, or his donkey, or anything that is your neighbor's."

Deuteronomy 5.21

> "'And you shall not covet your neighbor's wife. And you shall not desire your neighbor's house, his field, or his male servant, or his female servant, his ox, or his donkey, or anything that is your neighbor's.'"

Luke 12.13-21; Ephesians 5.5; Colossians 3.5; 1 Timothy 6.6-8

The Fellowship of Ailbe

The Fellowship of Ailbe is a spiritual order in the Celtic tradition, dedicated to advancing the rule of Christ in and through churches by working for spiritual enrichment and mutual encouragement among church leaders. The Fellowship offers a variety of services, including friendships, mentoring, training materials, seminars and retreats, and other resources available at its website www.myparuchia.com. Register to receive our daily email devotional, *Crosfigell*.

www.ingramcontent.com/pod-product-compliance
Lightning Source LLC
LaVergne TN
LVHW011412080426
835511LV00005B/499